The Bear

by Jess Roberts

PEARSON

Scott
Foresman

Editorial Offices: Glenview, Illinois • Parsippany, New Jersey • New York, New York
Sales Offices: Boston, Massachusetts • Duluth, Georgia • Glenview, Illinois
Coppell, Texas • Sacramento, California • Mesa, Arizona

The bear likes to play.

The bear likes to climb.

The bear likes to swim.

The bear likes to run.

The bear likes to drink.

The bear likes to eat.

The bear likes to sleep.